KIDS' FUNNIEST JOKES

Edited by Sheila Anne Barry

THESE JOKES REALLY GET MY **GOAT**!!

HE'S JUST KIDDING!

Illustrated by Jeff Sinclair

Sterling Publishing Co., Inc. New York

Library of Congress Cataloging-in-Publication Data

Kids' funniest jokes / edited by Sheila Anne Barry ; illustrated by Jeff
Sinclair.
     p.   cm.
    Includes index.
    Summary: An illustrated collection of classic riddles and jokes
contributed by children ages six and up.
    ISBN 0-8069-0449-6 (trade). — ISBN 0-8069-0448-8 (pbk.)
    1. Riddles, Juvenile. [1. Riddles. 2. Jokes.] I. Barry, Sheila
Anne. II. Sinclair, Jeff, ill.
PN6371.5.K53 1993
818'.540208—dc20   93-23045
                                                 CIP
                                               AC

21 20 19

Published by Sterling Publishing Co., Inc.
387 Park Avenue South, New York, NY 10016
Text © 1993 by Sterling Publishing Co., Inc.
Illustrations © 1993 by Jeff Sinclair
Distributed in Canada by Sterling Publishing
c/o Canadian Manda Group, 165 Dufferin Street
Toronto, Ontario, Canada M6K 3H6
Distributed in Great Britain and Europe by Chris Lloyd at Orca Book
Services, Stanley House, Fleets Lane, Poole BH15 3AJ, England
Distributed in Australia by Capricorn Link (Australia) Pty. Ltd.
P.O. Box 704, Windsor, NSW 2756, Australia

Sterling ISBN 0-8069-0448-8 Paperback

Contents

1. That's Life!

Who writes nursery rhymes and squeezes oranges?
Mother Juice.   RYAN BURKE, 10

Why was Newton surprised when he was hit on the head by an apple?
He was sitting under a pear tree!

GINA MORGAN, 8

"Mommy, mommy, what color are pears?"
"Green."
"Whoops, I just ate a lightbulb!"   PAUL WRIGHT, 9

What happened to the camper who swallowed the flashlight?
He hiccupped with delight (the light).

ADAM BRIGDEN, 9

KAREN: I can blow up 100,000 balloons a minute!
ANGIE: You're full of ballooney!   TIIU VAIL, 10

Why did the girl eat bullets?
So she could grow bangs.   ASHLEY WEISS, 8

Why did the firecracker go to the barber shop?
To get its bangs cut.   NATALIE LUSHMAN, 5

Where does a lamb go for a haircut?
To the baa-baa shop.   LISA CHEN, 9

What do witches put on their hair?
Scare-spray.   JENNIFER McCUMBER, 8

What does a monster call his parents?
Mom and dead.   MELISSA LINK, 10

Two girls are walking down the street. They look alike, have the same mother and father, and were born at the same time. But they are not twins. What are they?

They are triplets; the other sister stayed at home.

KEVIN TEIXEIRA, 7

"Who gave you that black eye?"
"Nobody gave it to me. I had to fight for it."

DUSTIN LEFFLER, 10

Who won the fight at the candy store?

I don't know, but the lollipop got licked!

MADONNA FRENCH, 8

Two tomatoes were walking to the park. One tomato was getting tired of walking, so he said to the other tomato, "Go along without me. I'll ketchup."

LEAH MORRIS, 9

What has two hands but can't wave?

A clock.   ALEX FIKIRIS, 6

How do you know that a clock is hungry?

It goes back for seconds.   REBECCA CONLY, 9

Why was the clock sad?

It had no one to tock to.   BETHANY HELMINK, 6

What do clocks say on Halloween?

"Tick or treat!"   KRISTY McDOUGALL, 9

What would you get if you crossed a nut and a briefcase?

A nut case.   ELENA ANDREWS, 10

What do you call a man who was born in Spain, raised in Africa, got married in Hawaii, and died in San Francisco?

Dead.

CHERYL DALEY, 7

"I had a terrible night. I dreamed I ate a fifty pound marshmallow."

"So what's so terrible about that?"

"When I woke up, my pillow was gone!"

JULIE LAMKEY, 7

What kind of bed is only good for three seasons?

One with no springs.   LAUREN PAUTLER, 11

GLEN: Mom, can Cathy and I go to the game?

MOM (*correcting him*): *May* Cathy and I go to the game?

GLEN: Sure! As long as I can go, too.

AARON BINNING, 10

What button do you always carry with you?
Your belly button.   COLLY NORMAN, 7

Why isn't your nose 12 inches long?
Because then it would be a foot.
                          HEATHER BOYLE, 9

"Can you give me a room and bath?"
*"I can give you a room, but you'll have to take your
own bath!"*   JHERMANE BARNES, 9

"Mommy, does God use our bathroom?"
"No, darling, why do you ask?
"Because every morning Daddy bangs on the door
and shouts, "Oh, God, are you still in there?"
                          PAUL TRISOLINI, 6

Why did the boy cut a hole in his umbrella?
So he could see when it stopped raining.
                          HILLARY FLEWELLING, 9

Did you hear the joke about the hole?
Never mind, you wouldn't dig it.
                          TAMMY JOHNSTON, 9

How much sand would be in a hole one foot long,
one foot wide, and one foot deep?
None, silly, there is no sand in a hole.
                          VICKY CABEL, 5

Ask your friend, "How do you spell silk? Your
friend will say, "S-I-L-K." Then ask your friend,
"What do cows drink?" 99.9% of the time your
friend will say "Milk." But cows drink water and
make milk. Try it!   JACQUELINE BERNARDI, 9

Why was the little boy surprised when he found cucumbers growing out of his ears?
Because he planted carrots.   JENNIFER KANG, 9

Is it okay to eat carrots with your fingers?
No, eat your carrots first, then eat your fingers.
CHRIS MOORE, 10

What do you get when you cross a banana peel with a banana peel?
A pair of slippers.   DANIELLE DREDGE, 7

Why is a bride sad on her wedding day?
She doesn't get to marry the best man.
STEPHEN POLLACK, 9

What do you call a baby who is learning to talk?
A little word processor.   ROB BRISTOW, 10

Why wouldn't the band leader go outside in the thunderstorm?
Because he was a good conductor.
SEAN JORGENSEN, 11

What would you get if you crossed a mummy with a CD?
A wrap (rap) song.   CHRIS DONISON, 9

What room don't skeletons like?
Living rooms.   CARLA WARD, 9

Who was the skeleton in the closet?
The winner of last year's hide and seek game.
TERINNA WALTERS, 10

What would you get if you crossed a snowball with a werewolf?

Frost bite. JORDAN WILSON, 10

Why didn't the skeleton go to the masquerade ball?

Because he had no body to go with.

SHAWN McPHAIL, 9

Why did the Post Office charge the goblin for his parcel?

It was ghost-marked C.O.D.

JAMES ECCLESTONE, 7

What did the little ghost have in his rock collection?

Tombstones. RACHELLE GAGNON, 10

What does a witch ask for when she checks into a hotel?

Broom service. CRYSTAL RAPOSO, 9

Why do vampires brush their fangs?
Because they don't like bat breath.

STEPHANIE McPHAIL, 9

Why did Dracula go to the doctor?
Because of his coffin.   BRENNA JOHNSTON, 7

What is the difference between a hill and a pill?
A hill is hard to get up. A pill is hard to get down.

KRISTEN PARSONS, 7

What kind of candy do you eat when you are about to die?
Life Savers.   DISHNA KIRIELLA, 8

BABY SNAKE: Mommy, am I poisonous?
MOTHER SNAKE: No, why?
BABY SNAKE: Because I bit my tongue!

COLE BURTON, 9

What is white and lifts weights?
An extra-strength aspirin.   CHRIS WALKER, 9

What's red and red and red all over?
A measle with a sunburn.   DANIEL BALMENT, 11

Why does a banana use suntan lotion?
So it won't peel.   AMANDA CASSIDY, 7

"Doctor, I think I'm a pin."
"Yes, I think I see your point."
JESSICA KAVANAGH, 7

"Doctor, I only have thirty seconds to live!"
"I'll be with you in a minute."   DEREK TAPHOUSE, 10

My doctor gave me six months to live. But I couldn't
pay the bill, so he gave me another six months.
DAVE PURA, 11

Why was the clock put in the hospital?
It was a little cuckoo.   TIM TRIBBLE, 7

Where do sick horses go?
To a horspital.   CATHERINE JOHNSON, 8

Where do you take a sick kangaroo?
To a hopital.   ASMA KHAN, 10

What do you do with a seasick elephant?
Give it lots of room.   ANDREW QUEEN, 7

Where are dead Martians listed?
In the orbit-uaries.   LANDON PINCOMBE, 10

Why don't blind people skydive?
Because it scares the living daylights out of their dog.

REBEKAH ORMSTRUP, 11

Why didn't the dog talk to his foot?
It's not polite to talk back to your paw.

ADELE ARMSTRONG, 10

MAN: I want to try on that suit in the window.
CLERK: Sorry, sir, but you'll have to use the dressing
    room.   KATHERINE FRANEY, 7

What do you call fear of tight chimneys?
Santa Claus-trophobia.   TIM O'BRIEN, 7

What do you get when you cross Santa Claus with
a cat on the beach?
Sandy claws.   KARLA CHISHOLM, 10

Why does Santa Claus have a big garden?
Because he likes to ho-ho-ho!   ANDREW WALKER, 8

One day a boy went to the day care center, but
he hated it so much he crawled out the window.
When he was out, he yelled, "I'm free!" Just then a
little girl came up to him. "So what," she said,
"I'm four!"   SAM SHEPARD, 10

What is a ghost's favorite car?
Boo-icks.   CHRISTIE FURLONG, 9

What kind of car has whiskers and purrs?
A Cat-illac.   SARAH GUNTHER, 10

How many wheels does a car have?
Five, with the steering wheel.

     CARLOS HUARCAYA, 9

What happens when you go in front of a car?
You get tired.

What happens when you go in back of a car?
You get exhausted.

     MELANIE RUTHERFORD, 11

When are roads unpleasant?
When they are crossroads.

     MELISSA DE BENEDETTI, 10

What's the difference between a TV and a
newspaper?
Have you ever tried to swat a fly with a TV?

     TANIA STEININGER, 10

There once was a ferocious lion who ate a very large bull. He was so proud that he roared and roared until somebody shot him. The moral is: When you're full of bull, keep your mouth shut.

JESSIE YOUNG, 10

Why can't a bicycle stand?
Because it's two-tired. MICHAEL KILPATRICK, 10

How did the farmer count his cows?
With a cow-culator. EUGENE GUNN, 11

What's underneath every robot?
Its robot-tom. AMANDA KEUHL, 10

What days are strong days?
Saturday and Sunday. All of the other days are weak (week) days. DANNY LOPES, 10

What days of the week do monsters like best?
Moan-day, Tombs-day and Fright-day.

JOEY McMILLAN, 7

Why did Grandma have roller skates put on her rocking chair?
So she could rock and roll. SARA WALSH, 9

What goes 99-thump, 99-thump?
A centipede with a wooden leg.

KEANNE WUSATY, 9

2. Very Wild!

What do you get when you cross a werewolf with a dozen eggs?
A hairy omelet.   MICHELLE MIDDLETON, 10

What has fur and flies?
A dead werewolf.   MARK LOYNS, 8

What kind of monkey flies?
A hot-air baboon.   CHERYL LOU SUPAH, 8

Why can't leopards play hide and seek?
They're always spotted.   ERIN JAMISON, 10

What animals can you never trust?
A lion and a cheetah (cheater).   ALISON WILSON, 10

What goes clunk-clunk, squash-squash, clunk-clunk?
An elephant with wet sneakers.

PARCY BARTLETT, 7

Why did the elephant paint his toes white?
So he could hide in a chalk box.

DEBORAH SPEER, 8

Why didn't the elephant take a suitcase on vacation?
Because he already had a trunk.

TEDDY DIETRICH, 6

What's the difference between elephants and fleas?
Elephants can have fleas, but fleas can't have elephants.

KIRAN SANDHU, 9

Why don't elephants smoke?
Because their butts are too big to fit in the ashtray.

ADAM DENNERLEY, 8

How long does it take an elephant to eat a tire?
A good year (Goodyear). MATT KELLER, 8

Why is the elephant ride so much cheaper than the pony ride?
Because the elephant works for peanuts.
LAURIE ANNE OULTON, 9

Why was the elephant sitting on the marshmallow?
So he wouldn't fall into the hot chocolate.
MELODY TITUS, 10

What do you get when you cross a Volkswagen and an elephant?
A rabbit with a trunk. ASHLI OTT, 9

"What's the difference between an elephant and a loaf of bread?"
"I don't know."
"Then it's no good sending you to the store!"
CRAIG WELLS, 7

What do you get if you cross a monster and a freezer?
A dragon that breathes ice cubes.
STEPHANIE LeBLANC, 7

What do you get when you cross a crocodile with baloney?
A croco-baloney! LISA ANN PARKER, 10

DEER: Will you be a deer and lend me some doe?
BEAR: How much?
DEER: Oh, a buck or two.
BEAR: I can't bear this! EMILY LEROUX, 6

One day as a man was walking through the woods he came face to face with a bear. The man said, "Oh Lord, let this bear be Christian." Then he heard the bear say, "Oh, Lord, thank you for this food."

JAYME MACLELLAN, 10

Where do bears go on vacation?
Bear-muda.   BRENNA CONRAD, 8

Why are camels hard to see in the desert?
Because they are camel-flaged.   ERIN WISE, 10

What is black and white and blue?
A zebra that is very cold.   ROBBIE FOGAL, 8

How do you hide a rhinoceros?
Paint its horns yellow, and put it in a banana tree.
CHELSEY BOWTELL, 7

What shark can help you build a house?
A hammerhead shark. DARRIN GOSSE, 6

Do sharks like to act in movies?
Only if they get big, juicy parts.

CRYSTAL PORTER, 7

If a very small fish married a young dog, what would their baby be called?
A guppy puppy. BRITTANY WILLIAMSON, 7

What's green, then yellow, then green, then yellow?
A turtle rolling down a hill. TOM ZAK, 11

SHE: You remind me of the ocean.
HE: You mean I'm deep, strange and wild?
SHE: No, you make me sick. ROBBIE MCBURNEY, 9

If eight watches were stolen from a jewelry store, what criminal would the police look for?

An octopus who is never late.

ADAM McCALLUM, 6

What would you get if 200 centipedes fell into the ocean?

20,000 Legs (Leagues) Under the Sea.

NATHAN MUISE, 5

Why did Columbus sail the ocean?

Because he couldn't swim. JOSEPH HAJEK, 11

Why did the lamb go swimming?

It needed a baa-th. ERIN MEDAKOVIC, 9

Where do skeletons like to swim?

In the Dead Sea. JESSE COTE, 8

Where do cats like to swim?
In the Puss-ific.   CASEY HOGGARD, 9

What do you call a cat that swims in the ocean?
An octo-pus.   JORDAN ATKINSON, 8

What do you get when you cross a mink with an octopus?
A coat with eight sleeves.   MANDY MORGAN, 7

What's the difference between a whale and a cookie?
Have you ever tried dipping a whale in milk?
    JOHN HICKEY, 8

Where do fish put their money?
The river bank.   CANDICE HARDY, 10

Why did the two fish get married?
Because they were hooked on each other.
    KRISTINA ZINGER, 6

Where do fish sleep?
In waterbeds.
    ELIZABETH BOJKOVSKI, 9

Why did the black catfish come to the beach at night?
He was looking for a sand-witch.
    DEVON ZACHARY, 7

TOURIST: Are there any alligators around here?
NATIVE: Nope.
TOURIST *(diving into the water)*: Glad to hear it.
NATIVE: Not since the sharks came and scared them
      away.   STACEY FAYANT, 10

23

Why did the dinosaur eat the factory?
Because he was a plant eater.　　　TARYN GEE, 7

What do you get when dinosaurs crash their cars?
Tyrannosaurus wrecks.　　　BOBBI MOORE, 7

What would you get if you crossed a Tyrannosaurus Rex with a rose?
I don't know, but I wouldn't try smelling it!
　　　CHRISTINA HAXTON, 7

One day a girl answered the phone. A voice said, "I am the viper." She hung up. A minute later the phone rang again. The voice said, "I am the viper." She hung up. A few minutes later, the doorbell rang. The man said, "I am the viper. I came to vipe and vash your vindows."　　　KATE O'DONOGHUE, 9

3. Knock-Knock!

Knock-knock.
  Who's there?
Abbey.
  Abbey who?
Abbey birthday!
            KIERA PARTON, 8

Knock-knock.
  Who's there?
Adam.
  Adam who?
Adam my way.
        JEFFREY CHEVRIER, 11

Knock-knock.
  Who's there?
Adolph.
  Adolph who?
Adolph (a golf) ball hit me
and now I talk like dis!
     JENNIFER VERBEKE, 11

Knock-knock.
  Who's there?
Amanda.
  Amanda who?
Amanda (A man to) fix
the TV.
      KIMBERLY MORRISON, 8

Knock-knock.
  Who's there?
Aldo.
  Aldo who?
Aldo anything for you.
      NADEEN MOHAMMED, 7

Knock-knock.
 Who's there?
Alfred.
 Alfred who?
Alfred (I'll thread) the needle if you sew on the button.
CHRISTINA ELLERBY, 11

Knock-knock.
 Who's there?
Amos.
 Amos who?
Amos-quito is buzzing around your head.
JASON NICKERSON, 6

Knock-knock.
 Who's there?
Anna.
 Anna who?
Anna-other mosquito.
STEPHANIE BLACKBURN, 9

Knock-knock.
 Who's there?
Andrew.
 Andrew who?
Andrew (Ann drew) on the wall—she's in big trouble!
KATHRYN ZANGARI, 10

Knock-knock.
 Who's there?
Andy.
 Andy who?
Andy green grass grows all around.
KATHRYN DUFFY, 9

Knock-knock.
 Who's there?
Annie.
 Annie who?
Annie body home?
PATRICIA TAILLEFER, 11

Knock-knock.
  Who's there?
Arthur.
  Arthur who?
Arthur any more knock-knock jokes?
  DANICA HOLLENDER, 7

Knock-knock.
  Who's there?
Barbie.
  Barbie who?
Barbie Q. Chicken.
  BECKY HOLOWUYCHUK, 9

Knock-knock.
  Who's there?
Canoe.
  Canoe who?
Canoe come out and play?
  JACKIE BROWNING, 10

Knock-knock.
  Who's there?
Cargo.
  Cargo who?
Cargo beep-beep.
  STEPHANIE POLSON, 10

Knock-knock.
  Who's there?
Catsup.
  Catsup who?
Catsup a tree—quick call the fire department!
  JOHN BRANCELA, 8

Knock-knock.
  Who's there?
Cook.
  Cook who?
Hey, who are you
calling cuckoo?
                BRYAN RIOS, 10

Knock-knock.
  Who's there?
Cows go.
  Cows go who?
No, cows go "moo."
                LAURA GALLANT, 9

Knock-knock.
  Who's there?
Danielle.
  Danielle who?
Danielle, I heard you
the first time!
                JONATHAN LOUIE, 8

Knock-knock.
  Who's there?
Dewey.
  Dewey who?
Dewey have to tell
knock-knock jokes now?
                AMANDA McGUIRE, 8

Knock-knock.
  Who's there?
Doe.
  Doe who?
Doe Nut!
                LARISSA CHALMERS, 11

Knock-knock.
  Who's there?
Doughnut.
  Doughnut who?
Doughnut come near
me. I have a cold.
  CHRISTINA MONGE, 10

Knock-knock.
  Who's there?
Duncan.
  Duncan who?
Duncan doughnuts
makes them soggy.
  PAMELA GOERTZEN, 10

Knock-knock.
  Who's there?
Dustin Hoffman.
  Dustin Hoffman who?
Dustin Hoffman (off my) pants.
  STEPHANIE HILLIER, 12

Knock-knock.
  Who's there?
Eileen.
  Eileen who?
Eileen over and
I fall down.
  RICKI FOUCAULT, 9

Knock-knock.
  Who's there?
Ether.
  Ether who?
Ether Bunny.
  SARAH BROWN, 10

Knock-knock.
  Who's there?
Europe.
  Europe who?
Europe-oo (you're
a poo) too!
  SHILOH PETER, 9

Knock-knock.
  Who's there?
Fanny.
  Fanny who?
Fanny-body calls, I'm out
of here!
  JOSH BIBBY, 6

Knock-knock.
Who's there?
Ghost.
Ghost who?
Ghost-and (go stand)
in the corner.
ADAM PAXTON, 9

Knock-knock.
Who's there?
Goblin.
Goblin who?
Goblin your food will
make your tummy ache.
MIKE VALLEE, 8

Knock-knock.
Who's there?
Gorilla.
Gorilla who?
Gorilla me a cheese
sandwich, please!
DREW CHENIER, 4

Knock-knock.
Who's there?
Hans.
Hans who?
Hans up! It's a
robbery!
HARMON LEE, 11

Knock-knock.
Who's there?
Handsome.
Handsome who?
Handsome popcorn over
here please!
STEPHANIE UHRIN, 7

Knock-knock.
Who's there?
Harry.
Harry who?
Harry up and let me in.
LEANNE BERGER, 9

Knock-knock.
Who's there?
Hatch.
Hatch who?
God bless you!
BRIAN BERNARDI, 7

Knock-knock.
  Who's there?
Heaven.
  Heaven who?
Heaven you heard this one before?
JAMIE McMILLAN, 8

Knock-knock.
  Who's there?
Henrietta.
  Henrietta who?
Henrietta worm that was in his apple.
JAMIE LAROSE, 9

Knock-knock.
  Who's there?
Honeycomb.
  Honeycomb who?
Honeycomb my hair.
MARICEL CABILAN, 10

Knock-knock.
  Who's there?
Howell.
  Howell who?
Howell I get in if you don't open the door?
KIMBERLY HALL, 8

Knock-knock.
  Who's there?
Ice.
  Ice who?
Ice-ee (I see) you.
LINDSEY MALLAIS, 8

Knock-knock.
  Who's there?
Ida.
  Ida who?
Ida left if you hadn't answered the door!
ERIN MAXNER, 7

Knock-knock.
  Who's there?
I don't know.
  I don't know who?
Neither do I.
  NADINE MICHELLE HOWICK,
                          10

Knock-knock.
  Who's there?
Justin.
  Justin who?
Justin time for dinner.
           SHERNAZ PAURI, 9

Knock-knock.
  Who's there?
Iraq.
  Iraq who?
Iraq my brains to think
up knock-knock jokes!
         BRIAN JOHNSON, 10

Knock-knock.
  Who's there?
Koala.
  Koala who?
Koala for help—the
house is on fire!
           KEN STOREY, 6

Knock-knock.
  Who's there?
Lettuce.
  Lettuce who?
Lettuce in and you'll see.
  SAMARJIT PARMAR, 10

Knock-knock.
  Who's there?
Luke.
  Luke who?
Luke—I'm standing
on my head!
  RYAN BONNAR, 7

Knock-knock.
  Who's there?
Midas.
  Midas who?
Midas well relax, no
school all summer.
  NADINE CHIEF, 10

Knock-knock.
  Who's there?
Matthew.
  Matthew who?
Matthew (my shoe) lace
is untied.
  MATTHEW KONIECZNY, 7

Knock-knock.
  Who's there?
Noah.
  Noah who?
Noah good knock-knock
joke?
  SCOTT TRACEY, 10

33

Knock-knock.
  Who's there?
Oldies.
  Oldies who?
Oldies chips give
me a stomachache.
KIMBERLY LAVALLEY, 6

Knock-knock.
  Who's there?
Olive.
  Olive who?
Olive us are cold.
PHILIP WOLFKAMP, 9

Knock-knock.
  Who's there?
Owl.
  Owl who?
Owl I get to sleep with
all this knocking?
JOHN FIDDY, 8

Knock-knock.
  Who's there?
Olga.
  Olga who?
Olga home if you treat
me this way!
GRACE ZAMORA, 8

Knock-knock.
  Who's there?
Owen.
  Owen who?
Owen are you going to
open the door?
JAMILYN BROWN, 7

KNOCK
KNOCK
KNOCK

Knock-knock.
  Who's there?
Peas.
  Peas who?
Peas (pleased)
to meet ya!
          KELSEY TREVORS, 8

Knock-knock.
  Who's there?
Philip.
  Philip who?
Philip my cup.
          IVY QUICHO, 9

Knock-knock.
  Who's there?
Panther.
  Panther who?
Panther no pants, I'm
going swimming.
          SHELLEY BERGER, 12

Knock-knock.
  Who's there?
Police.
  Police who?
Police stop telling me
these stupid knock knock
jokes!
          BRADEN SCHATZ, 10

Knock-knock.
  Who's there?
Queen.
  Queen who?
Queen your dishes or
you don't get any
dessert.
          ROBERT DORT, 11

Knock-knock.
  Who's there?
Rabbit.
  Rabbit who?
Rabbit up neatly—it's a
birthday present.
          ANGELA TATLA, 7

Knock-knock.
  Who's there?
Radio.
  Radio who?
Radio not—here I come.
  STEVE KOSTOVSKI, 10

Knock-knock.
  Who's there?
Rita.
  Rita who?
Rita lot of good books?
  AMANDA ST. PIERRE, 11

Knock-knock.
  Who's there?
Robin.
  Robin who?
I'm robin the rich and
I'm givin' to the poor.
  MATTHEW DORREN, 8

Knock-knock.
  Who's there?
Ron.
  Ron who?
Ron faster—there's an
alligator chasing us.
  ERIN ONOFRYCHUK, 9

Knock-knock.
  Who's there?
Ryan.
  Ryan who?
Ryan-oceros
(rhinoceros).
  AMY MCKEEN, 7

Knock-knock.
  Who's there?
Sarah.
  Sarah who?
Sarah (is there) someone
at the door?
  SARAH MCDOUGALL, 9

Knock-knock.
  Who's there?
Sherwood.
  Sherwood who?
Sherwood like to eat
lunch.
            RYAN RUSSELL, 11

Knock-knock.
  Who's there?
Shh.
  Shh who?
Fine, I'll go away.
            ELIZABETH TARON, 10

Knock-knock.
  Who's there?
Snakeskin.
  Snakeskin who?
Snakeskin (snakes can) bite.
        JACKIE HAGGARD, 8

STUDENT: Knock-knock.
PIANO TEACHER: Who's there?
STUDENT: Wendy.
PIANO TEACHER: Wendy who?
STUDENT: Wendy I get to
use the gas pedal?
        DANIELLE ANDREWS, 7

Knock-knock.
  Who's there?
Tank.
  Tank who?
You're welcome!
        JOEY KIPPING, 8

Knock-knock.
  Who's there?
Tiger.
  Tiger who?
Tiger (tie your) shoes or
you'll trip.
        BOBBY McCONNELL, 7

37

Knock-knock.
  Who's there?
Toodle.
  Toodle who?
Toodle who to you too!
COURTENAY ECCLESTONE,
8

Knock-knock.
  Who's there?
Watson.
  Watson who?
Watson T.V.?
DEXTER BRAITHWAITE, 11

Knock-knock.
  Who's there?
Wooden shoe.
  Wooden shoe who?
Wooden shoe like to
know!
AIYSSAM BLACK, 8

Knock-knock.
  Who's there?
Tuba.
  Tuba who?
Tuba toothpaste.
SAMANTHA GOETTEL, 7

Knock-knock.
  Who's there?
Ula.
  Ula who?
Ula-la (oo-la-la!)
NIRU MARIANAYANAGAM,
9

Knock-knock.
  Who's there?
Who.
  Who who?
Stop trying to imitate an
owl! This is a joke, not
an owl act!
JOSHUA DAY, 11

Knock-knock.
  Who's there?
Ya.
  Ya who?
Ride em', cowboy!
WILLIAM MITCHELL, 7

4. What Was That Again?

What did the bee say to the flower?
"Hello, honey!" KIM MARIE, 9

What did one earthquake say to the other earthquake?
"It's not my fault." CHRISTINE VILLENEUVE, 12

What did the beach say when the tide finally came in?
"Long time no sea!" CANDICE PORTER, 7

What did one wall say to the other wall?
"Meet you at the corner!" ZACHARY LUFT, 5

What did the paint say to the wall?
"Don't move—I've got you covered!"

DEVIN BROWN, 8

What did the shrimp yell to the seaweed?
    "Kelp! Kelp!"   JOSHUA FAST, 7

What did the boy octopus say to the girl octopus?
    "I want to hold your hand, hand, hand, hand, hand, hand, hand, hand."   CHANTELLE BARAN, 9

What do you say to a 40-ton shark with razor sharp teeth who is listening to his headphones with the volume turned way up?
    Anything you want, he can't hear you.
                                                    CODY STUMP, 9

What did the iguana say when he met the dinosaur?
    "Iguana go home."   BRANDON BENNETT, 9

What did the rake say to the hoe?
 "Hi, hoe!" MELISSA HOWLETT, 9

There were three men in a desert. The first man said, "I brought water in case we get thirsty." The second man said, "I brought bread in case we get hungry." The third man said, "I brought a car in case it gets hot, so we can roll down the windows."
JILL SMITH, 10

What did one clothesline say to the other clothesline?
 "You don't have any clothes on."
STEPHANIE LUSHMAN, 8

What did the baby chimney say to the father chimney?
 "Pop, you smoke too much." DAVID McLEAN, 9

What did one tombstone say to the other tombstone?
 "Don't take me for granite." SARA DAVIS, 13

What did the tie say to the hat?
 "You go on ahead, and I'll hang around."
BRONWYNN HEARD, 6

What do you say before you start a meeting with ghosts?
 "Please be sheeted." MATTHEW SCHNEIDER

PEG: What time is it?
MEG: I don't know.
PEG: What does your clock say?
MEG: Tick-tock, tick-tock. JUSTIN LONG, 9

What did one pink flamingo say to the other pink flamingo?

"Let's buy two pink people this year and put them on our front lawn." NINA SQUIRES, 9

What does a 500-pound parrot say?

"Polly wants a cracker, NOW!" TONY KELLY, 10

What did the cloud say to the banker?

"I'll take a rain check." DARREN RICHARDSON, 7

What did the policeman say to the shirt?

"You're under a vest!" CARRIE STINSON, 10

One day little Susie, age six, was complaining she had a stomachache. Her mom said that was because her stomach was empty. Later on she heard the pastor say he had a headache. Little Susie perked up and said, "That's because it's empty. If you had something in it, you'd feel better." LACEY WILSON, 11

What did the elephant say when the mouse stepped on his toe?

"Pick on somebody your own size."

HEATHER FREEMAN, 9

What did Hannibal say when he saw the elephants coming?

"Here come the elephants!"

What did Hannibal say when he saw the elephants coming with sunglasses on?

Nothing—he didn't recognize them.

JODY SMITH, 12

Say "iced ink," while plugging your nose.
(It will sound like you're saying, "I stink.")
JESSICA BURGESS, 11

What did the ocean say to the shore?
Nothing, it just waved!   BARRY MacKICHAN, 8

What did the man say when he saw the woman's painting?
"I'm going to have an art attack."

DARREN COINES, 9

What did one eye say to the other eye?
"Just between you and me, something smells."
GEOFFREY ROTH, 10

What did one candle say to the other candle?
"Are you going out tonight?"   TOMMY EVANS, 10

What did the monkey say when the train ran over his tail?

"*Won't be long, now!*" LISA SHEWCHUK, 8

While visiting a senior citizens' home, I approached one of the ladies and asked, "Are you Rose Long?" "No," she replied, "I just got up."

STEPHANIE EDISON, 8

What did the old man say when he walked into the antiques store?

"*What's new?*" STEPHANIE PAUL RICHARD, 11

What does a chicken say when he goes into a library?

"*Book-book-book-book-book!*" TASHIA LACROIX, 10

What did the little calf say to the mother cow?

"*I had to get a drink one way or the udder!*"

MARIA THOMAS, 9

What did the little lamb say to the mother sheep?
"I love ewe, maaamaaa!"   THERESA GIBSON, 8

What did the pony say when it had a sore throat?
"Excuse me, but I'm a little hoarse (horse)."
                                    AMY CHENG, 12

What do you say when your dog runs away?
"Doggone!"   CHANTEL WILMOT, 10

What did the scientists say when they found bones on the moon?
"The cow didn't make it."   THOMAS MORGAN, 8

What does Teddy Bear yell when he cuts down a tree?
"Tim-bear!"   CHRISTOPHER KROCK, 7

What did one garbage can say to the other garbage can?
Nothing. Garbage cans can't talk.
                                    EMMA SEMPLE, 7

What should you say to a one-year-old frog?
"Happy Birthday!"   ERIC KOCH, 6

5. What Could It Be?

What has two arms, two legs, always wears black and follows you everywhere?

Your shadow. DAWSON DEL TORCHIO, 11

What has four legs on one side and two on the other, and two heads?

A horse with a lady sitting sidesaddle.

TANIS MACALA, 9

What has four legs, four arms, four eyes, four ears, two heads, two noses, and two mouths?

A person with extra parts. MIKEL WITLOX, 7

I have eight eyes, four legs, six eyebrows, webbed fingers and my hair stands up. What am I?

Very ugly. CRYSTAL HARTY, 8

I don't have it; I don't want it. But if I had it, I wouldn't take the world for it. What is it?

A bald head. TRINA SCHROEDER, 9

What is yours and yet used by others more than by yourself?

Your name. CHRISTINE MARIE FARKAS, 11

What has red bumps and is the fastest gun in the west?

Rootin' tootin' raspberry. TYLER GREGORY, 8

What has twenty teeth and can't chew?

A comb. JEFFERY FEHRENBACH, 6

What has fifty teeth but can't chew?

A saw. AMANDA HEFFERNAN, 6

What do you lose when you stand up?

Your lap. ANDREA EDISON, 10

What has 100 legs and can't walk?

Fifty pairs of pants.

DARRYL ROBSON, 9

When is a car not a car?

When it turns into a driveway.

JOEL WAECHTER, 7

What's a skeleton's favorite road?

A dead end. MELISSA SHANNON, 11

What does a boy monster call a girl that has three eyes, two noses and three mouths?

Cute. STEPHANIE WONG, 7

"Tomorrow is my father's birthday."
"What are you going to give him?"
"Something better than last year."
"What did you give him last year?"
"Chicken Pox."   VIRGILIO ESTEBAN, 9

What word starts with an "E," but usually contains only one letter?
Envelope.   TRICIA PHILLIPS, 11

What has fingers but cannot use them?
Gloves.   ANDREW JONES, 6

What do you call a sleeping bag?
A knap sack.   MATTHEW TURNER, 6

What breaks but does not fall and what falls but does not break?
Daybreak and nightfall.

                                        JEFF FRANCIS, 11

What is something everyone has seen but will never see again?
Yesterday.   CHRISTINA REINHART, 11

What does a dyslexic, atheist insomniac do?
He stays up all night wondering if there is a Dog.
                                        JORDAN GROVES, 11

What do you call an oyster who doesn't let anyone share his pearl?
Shell-fish.   LEVON CADDY, 8

What grows between your nose and chin?
Tulips.   SARA ORCHARD, 8

What do you call a ghost that picks on other ghosts?

A boo-lly. EMILY SCAMMELL, 11

What kind of ghost plays cards?

A pokergeist (poltergeist). CRISTA HEWITT, 10

If I laugh, it laughs. If I cry, it cries. But if I turn around it won't laugh or cry. What is it?

A mirror. ANDREA ROMAN, 10

What do you call a cow with no legs?

Ground beef. MARK KOTELKO, 7

What's black and white and red on the bottom?

A zebra with a diaper rash.

CHRISTOPHER MONTGOMERY, 6

What's red and mushy and found between shark's teeth?

Slow swimmers. RYAN YOUNG, 11

What do you call a dog's kiss?
A pooch smooch. JENNIFER REGINBAL, 8

What has a head like a cat, a tail like a cat, legs like a cat, but is not a cat?
A kitten. KEVIN COLLINS, 8

What's as big as an elephant and weighs nothing?
An elephant's shadow. SAMUEL ZENGER, 8

What do you call a bear who cries a lot?
Winnie the Boo-hoo. EMILY HARLE, 9

Name a hopping creature that breaks into houses.
A robbit. CHRISTINA CHABOT, 9

What vehicle has four wheels and flies?
A garbage truck. KEVIN WONG, 10

What do you call a boomerang that doesn't come back?

A stick. JULIE MOFFAT, 8

What telephone company do canaries use for making bird calls?

A Tweet & Tweet. JENNIFER BOUCHARD, 8

Tie a knot in my neck and I'll be much more fun. What am I?

A balloon. RACHEL MCWILLIAM, 10

What do you get when you cross a tricycle with a joke book?

A yamahaha. RYAN FRY, 7

What's black and white and green?

Two skunks fighting over a pickle.

JAY BROCKBANK, 10

What has sixteen arms?

Two octopuses shaking hands. TREVOR SCHULTZ, 10

What ticks on the wall?

Ticky paper, tupid! JENNIFER COMEAU, 7

What do ants use for a hula hoop?

Fruit loops. SARAH KEYES, 9

What kind of grass pinches?

Crabgrass. JEFFREY BELL, 10

What do you call a snake and a long black car?

A hiss and a hearse. KRISTEN KLASSEN, 10

Where can a monster always find a friend?
In the dictionary. ANGELA NAUGLE, 11

What would you get if you crossed a person from Paris with lightning?
A french fry. HEIDI MacDONALD, 9

What would you get if you crossed a motorboat with a golfer?
A motorboat that goes putt, putt putt.
IAN ANDERSON, 9

What lives in Florida and California, is big and brown, and has antlers?
Mickey Moose. CHRISTINE ESSELMAN, 9

What is black and white and red all over?
A dalmatian with a sunburn.
LEAH SCHNURR, 10

What is black and white and yellow?
A bus full of zebras. MITCH WALKER, 8

What do you get if your stockings fall off, your ornaments break, and Santa tracks soot through your living room?
A merry Chris-mess. CARTER EDIE, 9

6. Back to School

Why does the letter A look like a flower?
Because a B always comes after it.

DEREK MACKY, 8

Why did the silly kid put his head on the grindstone?
To sharpen his wits.   STEVEN GELINAS, 9

Why did the boy bring the ladder to school?
He wanted to go to high school.

JULIE DESJARDINS, 9

TEACHER: Lisa, when was the Great Depression?
LISA: Last week when I got my report card.
          ANDREW STEVENSON, 9

What's the biggest room in the world?
Room for improvement.   JESSE SOCCHIA, 8

I happen once in every minute, but twice in every moment. I never happen at all in a hundred thousand years. What am I?

The letter "M."   MATTHEW WILLCOTT, 8

Why is six afraid of seven?

Because seven ate (eight) nine.

MARI-ANN THOMPSON, 10

TEACHER: Ted, if your father has ten dollars and you ask him for six dollars, how many dollars would your father have left?

TED: Ten!

TEACHER: You don't know your math.

TED: You don't know my father!

DARREN KLASSEN, 10

Why was the cannibal expelled from school?

For buttering up the teacher.   DAVID ROSSO, 10

What is a retired teacher?
One with no class and no principals (principles).

JARETT NICK, 6

PRINCIPAL: Only fools are positive.
STUDENT: Are you sure?
PRINCIPAL: I'm positive.

ROSA GIDORA, 10

Why didn't the teacher believe the ghost?
Because she could see right through him.

BRANDON SCHAUFELE, 7

How did the ghost teacher explain the lesson on going through a wall?
She went through it again and again.

AMANDA SCHAUFELE, 9

Do you know why they fired the cross-eyed teacher?
Because she couldn't control her pupils.

TIM RUNSTEDLER, 6

"What's the second to the last letter in the alphabet?
"Y."
"Because I want to know."

WYLON HYNNES, 7

Where do planets go to school?
The univers-ity.

TIM WERNER, 10

What word do people spell wrong?
Wrong.

RYAN MCLENNAN, 8

Roses are red, violets are blue,
I copied your test and I failed too.

JONATHAN GHEBREYOHANNES, 10

JIM: The teacher says we have a test today, rain or shine.

JOHN: Then why are you so happy?

JIM: Because it's snowing!

AMANDA SCHLUPP, 10

DAD: How were your test scores?

SON: Underwater, Dad.

DAD: What do you mean—underwater?

SON: You know, below C level!

DARLENE KLASSEN, 7

Now I lay me down to rest,
Pray I pass tomorrow's test.
If I should die before I wake,
That's one less test I'll have to take.

TYLER YOUNGS, 11

Why did they call the Middle Ages the Dark Ages?
Because there were so many knights (nights).

BEN INGRAM, 10

What's the biggest plant in the world?
The steel plant.   DOUG ROBINSON, 9

What are the names of the two favorite boys in school?
Gym and Art.   AMBER HRYNKIW, 10

What is a private eye's favorite subject?
Spience (science).   NATALIE BESSETTE, 9

Why did the class clown give Jenny a dog biscuit?
He heard she was the teacher's pet.

AMY RHYNO, 10

Why is it dangerous to do math in the jungle?
Because if you add four and four you get eight (ate).
NATHAN HUEBERT, 9

How does a monster count to 395?
On his fingers.　　　　　　RENNY CHAN, 11

What do you get when you cross a vampire with a pigmy?
A little sucker about this big.　　JANIS GAGNON, 8

Why is the vampire unpopular?
Because he is a pain in the neck!
HARLENE VIDALLO, 10

What Egyptian queen was a vampire?
Cleo-bat-tra.　　　　BRAMILEE DHAYANANDHAN, 10

TEACHER: What's half of eight?
ROBERT: Up and down or across?
TEACHER: What do you mean?
ROBERT: Up and down it's 3, and across it's 0.

ASHLEY CHURCH, 10

Who did the ghost take to the prom?
His ghoul friend. KERRY VISINSKI, 8

What's yellow, likes kids, and comes in the morning to brighten your mother's day?
A school bus. DAVID TAYLOR, 9

JOE: Why don't you take the bus home?
BEN: I can't. My mother would make me take it back. JONATHAN SEE, 9

What famous bus crossed the Atlantic?
Colum-bus. AARON WEBB, 10

TEACHER: Name three kinds of beans.
WILLIE: Lima beans, string beans, and human
    beings.   LEAH GRACE NONATO, 10

What did one textbook say to the other textbook?
  "Do you want to hear my problems?"
          MEGHAN STINSON, 8

JAMES: What's a student's favorite three words?
TEACHER: I don't know.
JAMES: Correct!   SHERRI HENDERSON, 9

What happened in 1492?
  I don't know, I was across the hall in 1493.
          MICHELE GEE, 12

TEACHER: Are you having a hard time with the
    questions?
STUDENT: No, just the answers!   MICHAEL FOX, 7

JOHN: I am not going to school, mom, because
    everybody laughs at me.
MOM: You have to go. You're the principal.
          JANET STUART, 11

7. How Do They Do It?

JIM: Did you hear about the guy who had his whole left side shot off?

SEAN: No!

JIM: He's all right now! DALE STEELE, 9

How could Goldilocks and the big bad wolf be in the same house?

It was a two-story house. AUSTIN NORTHCOTT, 9

How does the man in the moon cut his hair?

Eclipse it. ANGELA VILLENEUVE, 11

How do you discover the tightrope walker's secret?

By tapping his wire. DANA ENNIS, 8

How do you top a truck?

You tep on the brakes, tupid! CHAD RAWLING, 8

How do hockey players kiss?
They pucker up. LISA MOSER, 8

MOTHER: Johnny, how did you find school today?
JOHNNY: I got out of the bus and there it was.
MELISSA PAYNE, 11

What runs and runs and never moves?
A refrigerator. SAMANTHA CAMPBELL, 6

What can you drown in, but not get wet in?
Quicksand. DANIELLE KING, 9

What grows when it eats, but dies when it drinks?
Fire. LACEY SMITH, 9

What can you put in a barrel to make it lighter?
A hole. STEVEN HOUGEN, 7

There were three girls and they were walking to
school with an umbrella. How many girls got wet?
None. It wasn't raining. BOBBI JO NEUFELD, 10

What does somebody take before you get it?
Your picture. MARYANN BLAGDON, 6

"Do you have any gum?"
"No."
"Then how come your teeth are still in your
mouth?" OPHELIA HYLTON, 9

A passenger plane with 300 people on board
crashed over the Atlantic Ocean. Where would you
bury the survivors?
You don't bury survivors. SCOTT RASMUSSEN, 10

Those Blonde Jokes

Why does the blonde like cheese whiz?
Because it's got personality.

MEGHAN CHESTERMAN, 11

Why did the blonde put T.G.I.F. on her shoes?
T-oes G-o I-n F-irst.   JULIE LeBLANC, 12

How does a blonde hurt herself raking leaves?
By falling out of the tree.

JILLIAN DeWARE, 12

What do you call a bunch of blondes in a freezer?
Frosted flakes.   JENNIFER MORIN, 10

What did the blonde say when she saw Cheerios?
"Look—doughnut seeds!   PAMELA NIEMI, 10

How does a blonde kill a fish?
She drowns it.

How does a blonde
kill a bird?
She throws it off a cliff.   JASON WARD, 10

If a blonde and a brunette were to fall out of an airplane, who would crash first?
The brunette, because the blonde would have to stop and ask for directions.

CASSIE DAVISON, 10

How do bees get to school?
They wait at the buzz stop.

ETIENNE STOCKLAND, 5

You're the driver. Forty people get off the bus. Two people get on. A hundred more get on the bus and 12 get off. Forty more people get on and four get off. Who's the driver?
(The person who answers the question is the driver.)

LARA BRECHT, 10

How do you get a rest during gym?
Sit down on one of the laps.

SEAN REID, 11

What's the best way to force a couch potato to do situps?
Put the remote control between his legs.

ADAM BLAKELY, 10

JEFF: Mississippi is a very hard word, but I can spell it.

MOM: Ok, spell it.

JEFF: I-T! JEFFREY BROWN, 6

TEACHER: How old were you on your last birthday?

STUDENT: Seven.

TEACHER: How old will you be on your next birthday?

STUDENT: Nine.

TEACHER: That's impossible.

STUDENT: No it's not. Today is my birthday.

JAMIE SCHOEN, 10

Who's bigger—Mr. Bigger or Mr. Bigger's baby?
Mr. Bigger's baby, because it's a little Bigger.

LEE GILCHRIST, 9

How do you make a reindeer float?
Use one reindeer and two scoops of ice cream.

KIMBERLEY BURK, 9

How do you make a skeleton laugh?
Tickle its funny bone. COLLEEN CAVAT, 10

A girl was locked up in a room with only a bat and a piano. How could she get out?
There are two ways: She could swing the bat three times to get out, or use a piano key.
JOSEPH MACMICHAEL, 9

How can you tell if an elephant has been in your refrigerator?
There's a footprint in your cheesecake.
AMANDA EVANS, 11

How can you tell if an elephant has slept in your bed?
You look for peanut shells. STACY SCHWEIZER, 8

How does an elephant sink a submarine?
It knocks on the door. WALKER NEUMANN, 8

How many elephants can you fit into a small car?
Five—two in the front seat, two in the back, and one in the glove compartment. DEVIN PITTMAN, 10

How much does it cost for an elephant to get a haircut?
Five dollars for the haircut and 500 for the chair.
RACHEL IRWIN, 8

How do you catch a unique bunny?
Unique up on him.

How do you catch a tame bunny?
Da tame way. ASHLEE K. SAUNDERS, 9

How do you stop a skunk from smelling?
Plug its nose. SHAWN PRIMOSCH, 7

How do vampires travel?
By blood vessel. MATTHEW SIPCHENKO, 8

Reporter Interviews Captain Hook
Q. Captain, how did you get the wooden leg?
A. In a battle when a cannon ball struck my leg.
Q. And how did you lose your hand?
A. Also in a battle.
Q. Whatever happened to your eye? Surely you did not lose it in a battle as well?
A. Oh, no. I was on the deck of my ship when a seagull plopped on my eye.
Q. Surely that didn't take out your eye?
A. No, but it was the first day I had my hook.
STEVEN MONTI, 11

You're on an overnight hiking trip and you're facing north. On your right is the east and on your left is the west. What is at your back?

Your knapsack. JEREMY DeLONG, 10

What has four legs and can't walk?
A table. MARK HOYLES, 6

What walks on its head?
The nails in the sole of a shoe.
DEVRIN STONEHOUSE, 7

"If you were in line at a train ticket window and the man in front of you was going to Toronto and the lady in back of you was going to New York, where would you be going?"

"I don't know."

"If you don't know, then what are you doing in line?" KEVAN ST. JOHN, 10

What city are you in when you drop your waffle in the sand?

Sandy Eggo (San Diego)! JENNIFER SINCLAIR, 10

How did the police drive to the beach?
In a squid car. MATTHEW HEKKERT, 8

8. Food Frenzy

What do beavers eat for breakfast?
Oakmeal! STEVEN KRAEMER, 8

What do ducks eat for breakfast?
Quacker Oats. MICHELLE QUA, 11

What do sea monsters eat?
Fish and ships. LINDSAY DeGRAAF, 7

How are a grape and a squid alike?
They are both brown, except the grape.

TRACIE VUST, 11

"What hand do you butter your toast with?"
"Neither. I use a knife!" LAURA CRAWFORD, 9

What did one egg say to the other egg?
"Better get cracking!" A.J. HART, 7

What do astronauts eat on?
Flying saucers. JASON KOBELKA, 10

What do aliens eat for lunch?
Mars bars. AMY ENNS, 8

What does Frankenstein have for lunch?
About 2000 volts. JOEY REID, 10

What kind of food do snowmen eat?
Cold-slaw. MATT KENDRICK, 12

Why did the monster eat a lamp?
He wanted a light snack. CAITLIN CARSON, 8

What's a sheep's favorite snack?
A baa-loney sandwich. SAMUEL LEE, 9

What is Santa's favorite snack?
Peanut butter and jolly.
NATALIE CHARETTE, 7

What is an alien's favorite snack?
Martian-mallows. KAATRINA JENSEN, 8

What's a dog's favorite soup?
Chicken poodle. PAMELA FELHABER, 8

SALLY: Why is this soup green?
COOK: That's odd. It wasn't green when I
cooked it three weeks ago!
KATHRYN MacPHERSON, 9

What do ghosts eat for dinner?
Spook-etti. SHAWN DALY, 8

69

What's a ghost's favorite food?
I scream and boo-berry pie.   SCOTT McPHAIL, 11

What's the monster's favorite cafeteria food?
Grave-y.   TIMOTHY GELINAS, 10

What kind of cake do policemen like?
Cop cakes.   CHANTEL LAROCHELLE, 8

What is a stone cutter's favorite dessert?
Marble cake.   SIMON KING, 7

Why don't cannibals eat clowns?
Because they taste funny.
JEFFREY STROH, 6

What is blue, round, and wears a diaper?
A cold baby cranberry.   NATALIE MESSNER, 8

What's orange and crawls through the grass?
A wounded cheezy.   MICHAEL QUINN, 7

SON: Mom, I don't like the cheese with holes
in it.
MOTHER: Okay, just each the cheese and leave
the holes on the side of your plate.
VANESSA GARBUTT, 10

How do you make a strawberry shake?
Sneak up on it and say "boo!"
JACKIE BLANCHARD, 11

What did one raspberry say to the other raspberry?
"If you weren't so sweet, we wouldn't be in
this jam."   CHRISTINA PALUMBO, 7

What's black and white and red all over?
Dracula, after dinner.   JAMES SAYLER, 11

What's a vampire's favorite sandwich?
Boo-loney.   DENISE MUSHUMANSKI, 6

What do you get if you cross a bat with a banana?
A banana that hangs upside down.
                                    HAYLEE JOHNSON, 6

What did the baby banana say to the mother banana?
"I don't peel good."   ELAINE DUPUIS, 10

Did you hear about the two peanuts walking down the street?
One was a-salted (assaulted).
                                    MICHAEL BUENAVENTURA, 11

What kind of nuts have no shells?
Doughnuts.　　　　　　　　　　　　MICHAEL FARKAS, 7

What did the filling say to the doughnut?
It's jam packed in here.

CHRISTINE ROBERTS, 11

When should a doughnut chef quit?
When he is tired of the "hole" business.

NICHOLAS KING, 10

What kind of space villain works in a restaurant?
Darth Waiter.　　　　　　　　LEWIS ROBINOVITCH, 7

How did Ronald McDonald celebrate his marriage to
Wendy?
He gave her an onion ring.　　　DANIELLE DAMEL, 10

What happens if you cross an onion with a potato?
The potato starts to cry.

MARY ANN MacGEE, 9

What did Mary have when she went out for dinner?
Everybody knows that Mary had a little lamb.

REBECCA HOLLANDS, 9

KAREN: It's your turn to fix dinner tonight.
BILL: What happened? Did it break!

SANDY DHUDWAL, 9

What do you call the science of soda pop?
Fizz-ics.

SHAWNA McINALLY, 9

What starts with T, ends with T, and had T in it?
A teapot.

LORELIE FARKAS, 9

Why was the cook being mean to the food?
*Because he beat the eggs, whipped the cream
and mashed the potatoes.*

ERIN BELOUS, 10

What stays hot in your refrigerator?
A hot dog.

JENNY KELLY, 8

Where is the best place to eat a hamburger?
In your mouth.

MICHELLE MEGEVAL, 8

Where was the first french fry made?
In Grease.

SHAUN DEMPSEY, 9

What is the smallest room in the world?
The mushroom.

STEPHEN RADOS, 9

What is green and sings?
Elvis Parsley. M. GALLO, 9

With what vegetable do you throw away the outside, cook the inside, eat the outside, and throw away the inside?
Corn on the cob. HOLLY JARDINE, 9

Why don't lemons play in concerts?
They play too many sour notes.
MATTHEW PROCTOR, 11

Where do you learn to scoop ice cream?
At Sundae (Sunday) school.
ANDREW FISHER, 8

What is black and white and red all over?
A hot fudge sundae with ketchup.
LINDA WILLIAMS, 10

What dessert is cold and rings?
An ice cream phone (cone). KRISTIN LUKEY, 9

Why doesn't Garfield like tennis balls?
Because you can serve them, but you can't eat them. MELISSA TEE, 9

What's green on the inside, white on the outside and hops?
A frog sandwich. AMANDA AIKENS, 9

9. Work & Play

How does a snake get to work in the morning?
In hiss car. JUSTIN SMITH, 9

Why are barbers good drivers?
Because they know all the short cuts.
NATASHIA REDMOND, 8

What driver can't drive?
A screwdriver. EVE KRAJC, 10

FRIEND: What's the difference between a
jewelry salesman and a jail guard?
OTHER FRIEND: One sells watches and the
other watches cells.
CHANTELLE NADEAU, 8

75

How do you know a Slobovian has been to your computer?

There is white-out all over the screen.

CHRISTOPHER VANDERZEE, 11

What do you call a tire salesman?

A wheeler dealer.

DAVID SMITH, 9

Why did the teacher marry the janitor?

He swept her off her feet.

STEPHEN LaFORREST, 8

What do you call a fireman who loses his job?

A fired-man.

ALLISON GRAVES, 7

Why do tall people make better weathermen than short people?

Because short people are the last to find out when it's raining.

ANGELA HUNT, 8

When do astronauts eat?
At launch time. SAMANTHA THOMSON, 7

Two astronauts landed on a planet.
"Looks like Pluto," one said.
"How can you tell?" said the other one.
"From the bark, you silly." ANNA SIPCHENKO, 11

What do you call the Wright brothers if they make a mistake?
The wrong brothers.

SHAUN HASSANALI, 10

Where does a cow go on Saturday night?
To the moo-vies. MEGAN KANASKI, 9

What did everyone ask the butcher when the cat stole the meat?
"What's the matter—cat got your tongue?"

MICHAEL SWEEZEY, 9

How do you fire a librarian?
Throw the book at her. CATHLEEN THOM, 12

Why did the ball player bring rope to the game?
He wanted to tie the score. CHRIS WILSON, 8

What is the difference between a baseball player and his tired dog?
The ballplayer wears a uniform, the dog only pants. ELIZABETH MONAGHAN, 10

Why were the basketball players holding their noses?
Someone was taking a foul shot.

MARK WALER, 11

Three guys were playing cards in a graveyard. What did they say?

"We had better dig up another player."

THOMAS PARTLETT, 11

Where do ghosts play tennis?

On a tennis corpse.

KRISTIN HERNANDEZ, 8

Where do ghosts shop?

In boo-tiques.

JOYCLYN MENDONCE, 11

What music do Martians like to listen to?

Nep-tunes.

BRITANY SPARROW, 8

What pet can sing?

A trum-pet.

LUCA MASTROLONARDO, 11

What dance did the Pilgrims do?

The Plymouth "Rock."

NORA SEVERSON, 8

What do you call a group of musical chickens?
  A squawkestra.   CHANCE TAYLOR, 7

What would you get if you crossed a TV star with a pickle?
  Dill Cosby.   EMILEA JOURNAULT, 8

How many ears does Mr. Spock have?
  *Three. A left ear, a right ear, and the final
  front ear (frontier).*   JEFF YOKOM, 8

Why are E.T.'s eyes so big?
  He saw his phone bill.   JAY HEWITT, 8

One day a reverend decided to phone another reverend, so he called the operator. The operator asked, "Station to station?"
  "No," said the reverend, "Parson to parson."
                    ABIGAIL TIMKO, 12

Crossing the Road

Why did the chicken cross the road?
To lay it on the line. ELIZABETH KRUTHOF, 6

Why did the muddy chicken cross the road twice?
Because he was a dirty double-crosser.
SCOTT WALSH, 7

Why did the skeleton cross the road?
To get to the body shop. BRIAN NEDJELSKI, 10

Why did the bubble gum cross the road?
It was stuck to the chicken's foot.
PAUL MILLER, 10

Why did the turkey cross the road?
*Because the chicken retired and moved to
Florida.* DYNISE BRISSON, 8

Why did the dinosaur cross the road?
Because the chicken hadn't been invented yet.
JENNIFER SMITH, 8

Why did the cow cross the road?
To get to the udder side. IRENE RIESEN, 10

Why did the otter cross the road?
To get to the otter side. JESSICA NEIL, 10

Crossing the Road

Why did the chicken cross the road?
To see a man laying bricks. BERKLEY STAITE, 6

Why did the punk rocker cross the road?
He was stapled to the chicken.

MICHELLE DAVY, 12

Why did the bee cross the road?
To buy some bee-loney. COLBY ANDREW WISE, 9

Why did the chicken cross the playground?
To get to the other slide. JOHN ROY, 12

Why didn't the chicken cross the road?
Because Colonel Sanders was on the other side.

MICHELLE FITZGERALD, 8

Why did the chicken throw the record over the fence?
To listen to the other side. HELI ISOLEHTO, 11

Why did it take so long for the elephant to cross the road?
Because the chicken had trouble carrying him.

TAMARA LANE, 10

How did the egg cross the road?
It scrambled across. BREANNE STEPHENSON, 8

Why did the elephant have a lousy vacation?
Because the airline lost his trunk.   LISA CORMIER, 8

Why did the robber take a bath?
He wanted to make a clean getaway.
DAYNA SCHAAB, 8

Where does the king keep his army?
Up his sleeve-y.   KATHARINE M. SMITH, 9

There were three hunters going through the forest and they came upon these strange tracks. The first man said "These are moose tracks."
The second man said, "These are horse tracks."
But the third never got to say because he got hit by a train.   CASIE HALL, 10

Why did Sleeping Beauty sleep for a hundred years?
Because her alarm clock broke.   AMY BOS, 10

Why do witches fly on brooms?
Because vacuum cleaners are too heavy.
VIVIAN NG, 7

MOTHER: Oh, our dog drives me up the wall!
LITTLE GIRL: But mommy, our dog doesn't know how to drive!   KIMBERLEY WOODWARD, 7

What can a fisherman catch when it's raining?
A cold.   JAKE CUMMINS, 8

10. Animal Fair

What bird belongs in an insane asylum?
A loon-a-tic.   NATHAN LINKLETTER, 7

What kind of bird can lift up anything?
A crane.   ADAM SCANNT, 9

Why did the boy put a leash on his pet bird?
Because he wanted to be a jay walker.
                                                  CHANTIEL KLEMCHUK, 7

What do you get if a bird flies into your
lawnmower?
Shredded tweet.   RYAN BOULANGER, 9

Why do geese fly south in the winter?
Because it's too far to walk.
                                                  VICTORIA OREFICE, 8

I have the smartest dog in the world. When I ask him what is opposite of smooth, he answers "Rough."

CHRIS ANDERSON, 8

What's the difference between a whining kid and a whining dog at the door?

When you let the dog in, he stops whining.

BRADY SMITH, 12

What do you call a dog with no legs?

It doesn't matter. It won't come when you call it anyway.

COURTNEY ELLIOTT, 7

What do frogs do when they play baseball?

Catch flies.

JESSIE PHILIPPE, 11

What do frogs do when they play basketball?

They take jump shots.

MARTY FOX, 9

What do frogs drink at picnics?

Croak-acola.

BLAIR JACKIW, 6

What do frogs say when they clean windows?
"Rubbit, rubbit, rubbit."   JORDY YIM, 8

What movie are alien toads in?
"Star Warts."   BRADLEY WORONUK, 8

Why does a fly walk on the ceiling?
So he won't get stepped on.   BRADLEY FEICHT, 6

What lies on the ground, 100 feet up in the air?
A dead centipede.   SARAH NOFTELL, 10

What would you get if you crossed a centipede with a parrot?
A walkie-talkie.   LYNDSEY BURTENSHAW, 10

What insect can fight an entire colony of soldier ants and win?
Con-ant the Barbarian.   BRENT ALFRED, 9

What kind of insects are always polite?
Lady bugs.   COURTNEY MAYNE, 7

Why do spiders spin webs?
Because they don't know how to knit.

GAIL ANN MALLEY, 8

If there were three bees in a kitchen, which one would be the cowboy?
The one sitting on the range.

DOREEN KUMAR, 11

What would you get if you crossed a bee with a doorbell?
A hum-dinger!   MATTHEW HUEBERT, 9

What did the geese call their horror movie?
Poltergeese.

What did the chickens call their horror movie?
Poultrygeist. HILARY ZIELKE, 11

What do you get when you cross a rooster with a ghost?
A how do you dooooooo! KRYSTAL ROQUE, 9

Why do bats fly at night?
Because they're afraid to drive.
STEPHANIE ROBERTSON, 7

What do ducks put on their Christmas trees?
Duck-erations. CAMERON MacDONALD, 8

What is the difference between a football player and a duck?

One you find in a huddle, the other you find in a puddle. KYLE HENEY, 6

Why don't ducks like to get the mail?

They already have bills. CHRISTINE FEHRENBACH, 8

What is the difference between Donald Duck and an umbrella?

You can shut up an umbrella. DAVID ELIAS, 7

A duck, a skunk, and a frog went to a movie. Tickets cost one dollar. Which animal didn't get in?

The skunk. The frog had a green back, the duck had a bill, but the skunk only had a scent.

TYLER McNEIL, 8

What do you get when you cross an owl with a skunk?

An owl that smells bad but doesn't give a hoot. RHIANNON ROZIER, 9

What would you call a pre-historic skunk?

Ex-stinct.

DANIEL McCOWAN, 10

What's the difference between an egg and a skunk?

If you don't know, remind me never to send you to buy eggs. MELISSA ANDREWS, 8

How do you tell which end of a worm is its head?

Tickle its middle and see which end smiles.

ANDREW OLAVESON, 5

Where did the worm take his date?
To the Big Apple. ASHLEY MARIEN, 10

What do you get when you cross a raccoon and a gladiator?
A radiator. DIANNA WALLACE, 11

Why did the chipmunk stop arguing with the porcupine?
He got the point! ZAIBA ALI, 9

Why do squirrels spend so much time in trees?
To get away from all the nuts on the ground.
JACLYN MEDUID, 6

What do a cobra, a car, and a snowsuit have in common?
A hood. ADAM GOSSE, 8

What do you get when you cross a flea and a rabbit?
Bug Bunny. MEGAN ROBERTS, 10

Which rabbit stole from the rich to give to the poor?
Rabbit Hood. DARREN WILSON, 10

Which rabbits were famous bank robbers?
Bunny and Clyde. ROGER WILSON, 7

What kind of cars do rabbits drive?
Hop rods. MATTHEW NEVEU, 10

What do you get when you keep two rabbits under the hair dryer too long?
Hot cross bunnies. ANDREA SHILLOLO, 7

What's the difference between a cat and a comma?
*A cat has claws at the end of its paws, and a comma
has a pause at the end of its clause.*

JESSIKA CORMIER, 11

What is the best place in the universe for a thirsty
cat?
The Milky Way.   MICHELLE STONEY, 9

When is it bad luck to have a black cat cross your
path?
When you're a mouse.   AMBER SHINBINE, 10

How does a cat keep his breath fresh?
Mousewash.   VINCENT KING, 5

What do cats put in their hot chocolate?
Mousemellows!   SUZANNE MCCRACKEN, 10

What should you do if you wake up in the night and hear a mouse squeaking?

Oil it. PATRICIA STELNICKI, 9

What is the best way to catch a mouse?

Get someone to throw it to you.

EMERY WOLFE, 10

What kind of weather do mice hate?

When it rains cats and dogs.

MADISON SCHWARTZ, 7

Why should you wear boots in a pet store?

You might step in a poodle. JENNIFER STROH, 9

What does a poodle use to wash its fur?

Shampoodle. KRISTEEN AVILES, 10

Why was the poodle chasing his tail?
He wanted to make ends meet.

RYAN KARKKAINEN, 8

What dog has no tail?
A hot dog.

JENNY KARL, 7

What goes tick-tock-woof?
A watch dog.

BRAD HOLTZMAN, 10

If twenty dogs run after one dog, what time is it?
Twenty after one.

LOUISE THIBERT, 8

What do you do if the dog eats your homework?
Take the words right out of his mouth.

RYAN YULE, 8

"My dog has no nose."
"How does he smell?"
"Awful." ANGELA HOEPPNER, 11

KID 1: Hey, look. A bunch of cows.
KID 2: Not a bunch, a herd.
KID 1: Sure, I've herd (heard) of cows.
KID 2: No, a cow herd.
KID 1: So what if a cow heard? I didn't say anything
I wasn't supposed to.

ISAAC JENKINS, 8

What has one horn and gives milk?
A milk truck.

TROY CAMP, 11

Why does a cow wear a bell?
Because its horn doesn't work. AMY POWERS, 8

What would you get if you crossed a chicken with a cow?

Roost beef. CODY GREGORY, 8

What would you get if you crossed a cow with an octopus?

A cow that can milk itself. JASON MECHTL, 8

What would you get if you crossed a cow with a werewolf?

A hamburger that bites back.

TARA HOUGHTON, 10

What do cows put on their hamburgers?

Moo-stard and cow-chup. MICHAEL LUCAS, 7

What do you get if you cross a vampire with a cow?

Dracmoola. STEFANIE COLLETTE, 10

Why did the cow lie on the beach?
To tan her hide.   JOANNE BOYACK, 9

Why did the cow answer the telephone?
Because she wanted to co-moo-nicate.
                              TIMMY BOWERING, 6

Why did the farmer name his pig "Ink"?
Because it kept running out of the pen.
                              STACEY LUCHUCK, 10

Why shouldn't you tell a pig a secret?
Because it squeals too much.
                              BECKY PASTERNAK, 8

Do pigs make good drivers?
No, they're road hogs.   KRISTAPHER HARGRAVES, 7

What would you get if a pig learned karate?
Pork chops.   STEVEN ANDERSON, 8

What does a pig put on himself when he gets a burn?
Oinkment.   CHRIS SLACK, 7

What rolls in the mud and carries eggs?
The Easter pig.   JOEY DESORMEAUX, 6

Knock-knock.
  Who's there?
Dishes.
  Dishes who?
Dishes the end!

      SHELLEY BISHOP, 8

DISHES HEAVY.

Index

95

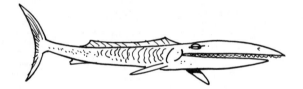